SURVIVING
your worst
FEAR

BONNIE BAKER

Christian Living Books, Inc.
An imprint of Pneuma Life Publishing
Largo, MD

ISBN 1-56229-211-0
ISBN13 978-1-56229-211-9

Christian Living Books, Inc.
An imprint of Pneuma Life Publishing, Inc.
P.O. Box 7584
Largo, MD 20792
301-218-9092
www.christianlivingbooks.com

Printed in the United States of America

Unless otherwise marked, all Scripture quotations are taken from the King James Version of the Bible.

DEDICATION

I dedicate this book in memory of my parents: my father, the late Mr. Jack Richardson, Sr.; my mother, the late Mrs. Clara Mae Richardson; and my father-in-law, the late Mr. Willie Baker, Sr. Also, to my first pastor, the late Apostle Charles O. Miles; my spiritual mother, the late Mother Mildred Poole; my grandmothers; all nine of my children; my two brothers, the late Jack Richardson, Jr., the late Clarence Richardson; my two brothers-in-laws, the late Pastor Lonnie J. White, the late Henry Peeples; my sister-in-law, the late Robin Baker; the late Deacon Johnny Hyman; two of my god children, the late Sada Williams, the late Darius Gilyard; and all other family members and friends. My love is with you.

CONTENTS

FOREWORD

In the past, God has used Evangelist Bonnie Baker to write her life story in her first book, *Then and Now.* That book revealed the awesome delivering power of God through steadfast intercessory prayer.

During this year of new beginnings, God has once again used Evangelist Bonnie Baker to write another awesome book: *Surviving Your Worst Fear.* The Bible states in 2 Timothy 1:7, "For God hath not given us the spirit of fear; but of power, and of love, and of a sound mind." I believe that this book will help those who are afraid of facing their fears. Evangelist Baker also has used her own personal experiences in the book to reveal how she overcame fear in her own life. This book will inform you how to apply the Word of God in your life to be victorious.

It is such a privilege and honor to know Evangelist Bonnie Baker personally. God has used her to be a blessing to our family and children for such a time as this.

This book shows how God has a purpose and a plan for our lives. Revelation 12:11 states, "They overcame him by the blood of the Lamb, and by the word of their testimony." After reading this book, I know you will be able to face your fears in Christ Jesus.

First Lady Carolyn Miles
International Gospel Center
Ecorse, Michigan

PREFACE

Ecclesiastes 3:1 states, "To every thing there is a season, and a time to every purpose under the heaven."

He hath made everything beautiful in His time. It is so wonderful to know that God knows us and watches over us, even as we were being formed in the womb.

What a blessing to know that God has a plan for our lives, a plan that He has known since before we were born. *Surviving Your Worst Fear* is a reminder that we are not alone. Just knowing this is a reminder that we can survive our worst fear when He is with us. He will never leave us. He will be with us in all our troubles.

It is such a blessed experience to be part of God's plan in bringing forth the knowledge of God.

In this book, *Surviving Your Worst Fear*, you'll discover that author Bonnie Baker is a living testimony of survival.

In knowing her for more than twenty four years, I've seen her struggle against many fears and watched her conquer and survive through prayer, fasting, and waiting patiently on God. This book will help the reader to trust God and mount up with wings as eagles. You will run and not be weary; you will walk and not faint (Isaiah 40:31).

Dr. Luvenia Miles
Founding First Lady
International Gospel Center

ACKNOWLEDGMENTS

I would like to thank my Lord and Savior, Jesus Christ, Who is the head of my life, for inspiring me to write this book.

To my husband, Dean, and my four daughters, Tawana, Kenyatta, Chantel, and Lachisa, thank you for all your love, prayers, and support, and for being there for me. I would not have made it without you. I love you so very much.

To my beloved pastor, Marvin N. Miles, and First Lady Carolyn L. Miles, thank you for your sweet inspiration, godly guidance, fervent prayer, and love. I love you.

To Dr. Luvenia Miles, thank you for all your love, prayers, teaching, hope, and encouragement. I love you.

To my sister Pastor Hattie P. White and church family at Redeeming the Times Ministries, thank you for everything and especially for all that you have done—the many, many phone calls, the many times you cried and laughed with me, all the prayers, the love and support. I really love you.

To my dear and sweet sister Barbara, I love you. Thank you for all you have done for me. But most of all, thank you for your love and support. And to all my other sisters, to all my brothers and all my brothers-in-law, all my sisters-in-law, my sweet mother-in-law, and all other family members, I really love you all.

To all my new mothers, I love you all so very, very much! Thank you for being there for me and for praying me through every time.

To my church family, International Gospel Center, thank you for all your prayers and support. You have been there for me through the years. God bless each and every one of you! I love you dearly.

To Marguerite Bird, thank you for all your help in everything. Thank you for your love, for your support, and for all your office help. I appreciate your kindness and your prayers. You are truly a blessing. I love you.

To my sweet daughters Kenyatta and Chantel, thank you for praying with me, typing, editing, taking pictures, and for everything you've done to help with this book. Mama loves you.

To all my beautiful god-children, I love you all.

To Kris Mathis, author of *From Drama ... to Destiny*, thank you for reading, editing, and helping with grammar. I love you.

To Christian Living Books, thank you for all your work in helping to make this book a success.

INTRODUCTION

Many times we are bound by fear and don't know why. However, I know God can deliver you from all your fears, doubt, and unbelief, for it has been said that you have nothing to fear but fear itself. You can overcome fear by asking God to remove it and then praising Him for His answer. Quote the Word of God about this, and He will give you provision and direction. In fact, the only safe place to be is in the will of God.

Many people face emotional stress and fear, which can cause sickness. But God let me know that He can free you from the deep fears you face on a daily basis. You can conquer your fear of rejection, your fear of failure, your fear of heights, your fear of dark places, your

fear of torment, your fear of flying, your fear of talking, your fear of making a mistake, your fear of causing an accident, your fear of being left alone, your fear of water, your fear of falling down, your fear of worrying, your fear of not fitting in, your fear of losing everything, your fear of wanting and not having, your fear of being fat, your fear of being small, your fear of low self-esteem, your fear of dying, and any other fears that may attack you.

Put the Word of God on it. Second Timothy 1:7 says, "For God hath not given us the spirit of fear; but of power, and of love, and of a sound mind." May this book be a blessing to you. Remember, beloved, love is the River of Life to the world; if you don't have love, you don't have anything. God bless you.

CHAPTER ONE

FEAR OF FEARS

What is fear? Fear is a personal emotional reaction you feel toward something, like the fear of God, and an emotional warning caused by the expectation or realization of danger. Although fear may be invisible, it is still real. It is a sudden feeling that we create ourselves, but it is true, we have nothing to fear but fear itself. The more you realize your fear, the smaller it gets, until you are left with the root of the problem that is causing you to have fear. Know that it can be dealt with and that you are a survivor of fear; you will outlast it, outlive it, and continue to exist.

Job said in Job 4:14, "Fear came upon me, and trembling, which made all my bones to shake." Job was a survivor. He went through the storm and came out, even though he had lost everything, and not once did he get upset with God.

> *And said, Naked came I out of my mother's womb, and naked shall I return thither: the LORD gave, and the LORD hath taken away; blessed be the name of the LORD.* (Job 1:21)

You see, Job lived through all his fear, and the very thing that Job feared the most came upon him. Remember, you have nothing to fear but fear itself.

> *For God hath not given us the spirit of fear; but of power, and of love, and of a sound mind.*
> (2 Timothy 1:7)

Remember, fear is a feeling and an emotional alarm or fright caused by the expectation of danger, pain, hurt, and so on. These are some of the fears we face every day:

- fear of someone never coming to see you
- fear of someone getting physically hurt or killed
- fear of making a mistake
- fear of feeling fear
- fear of always wondering what will happen
- fear of losing a loved one
- fear of being terrible

- fear of hearing a sound, an explosion, or a fearful noise, as in, "I think I heard something upstairs or downstairs."
- fear of being alone
- fear of thinking, *No one will ever love me*, and thinking, *I am always alone.*
- fear you yourself have caused for no reason
- fear of being found out: *Am I doing something wrong? Will I ever get caught? Will anyone ever find out?* We are not what we look to be when we are acting in fear.
- fear of being hurt in a love relationship, based on past hurt: *Will I ever love again?* and fear of who will have you: *I can never open up to anyone else again. Will I ever find the right one?*

Fear will have you shut yourself up in a box, never to come out again, and go on being upset, tangled up, tied up, and bound up with silent frustration. Then you can't trust anyone; there you will be left to live in hurt forever, until God brings you out. Other fears we commonly face are:

- fear of danger, always thinking something is unsafe or that someone will cause you injury or loss
- fear of falling, tripping, or falling down and getting hurt
- fear of heights: *I don't fly because I feel the plane will fall. I don't go to the fair or carnival because I fear the*

ride will fall apart. I don't like elevators because I fear they will stop and I may be stuck on them too high up. Anything that's

Fear of heights

up too high I fear. Just let me stay on the ground, and I will be all right. But remember, you have nothing to fear but fear itself. If you can get over the fear, you can make it!

- fear of death or dying, always thinking, *What if I die?* Remember, we all have an appointment with death, and fear comes and says: *When I go to sleep, I might not wake up. I am driving—will I lose control of the car? I remember the last accident I had. Will I die this time? If I go near water, will I drown?* This fear causes us always to think, *Will I die?*

Beloved, don't fear dying because it is appointed by God.

> *To every thing there is a season, and a time to every purpose under the heaven: a time to be born, and a time to die; a time to plant, and a time to pluck up that which is planted; a time*

to kill, and a time to heal; a time to break down, and a time to build up; a time to weep, and a time to laugh; a time to mourn, and a time to dance; a time to cast away stones, and a time to gather stones together; a time to embrace, and a time to refrain from embracing; a time to get, and a time to lose; a time to keep, and a time to cast away; a time to rend, and a time to sew; a time to keep silence, and a time to speak; a time to love, and a time to hate; a time of war, and a time of peace. (Ecclesiastes 3:1-8)

This Scripture tells us all about the "time of things." You see, this is the will of God for us—to be born and to die—so don't fear dying.

Fear of flying

CHAPTER TWO

CONQUERING YOUR FEARS

You can overcome fear, even the most irrational kinds that keep you from enjoying life and experiencing the normal Christian life that God has for us. In our Christian walk with God, one of the biggest fears we face is the fear of rejection. Rejection is very hard to deal with. This is because we all have a need to feel and accept love. Yet if we fear constantly, we will experience rejection. We always look at how people receive us and accept us, but this demonstrates the fear of rejection. We need to overcome our fear of rejection. In many cases, even Jesus was rejected by men.

He came unto his own, and his own received him not. (John 1:11)

You see, you can be rejected by your own. The best way to deal with rejection is to wait in the belief and love of God. We don't want to look for rest in the world, for the world is a lost generation, and we are the children of God. The way God sees you is more important than the way people see you. The overcoming grace of God will strengthen you and bless you with all the joy and peace needed when you are rejected by people. Since being rejected by people can be very hard to deal with, during that time of rejection, you need God to give you the grace to overcome all obstacles from rejection, fear, doubt, and unbelief.

Another type of fear is based upon failure, old age, illness, and death. We live in a day and time that the Bible tells us about: the last days. When the end comes, we know that it will be marked by great tribulations and trouble. And even then, many of God's people will still be facing fear and trying to get power over the fears that attack their lives. Let the Lord help you get past your fears.

> *Therefore, if any man be in Christ, he is a new creature; old things are passed away; behold, all things are become new.* (2 Corinthians 5:17)

Sometimes our past mistakes cause us to fear the future. However, the Lord wants the pain of our past to be gone so we can function without hurt and fear caused by past experiences. If you trust in God with all your heart, soul, and mind, then you can conquer and overcome the past fear—and the future fear—that may attack your mind. Remember, beloved, emotional stress and fear can cause sickness and pain in your body. The inner emotional healing from fear is sometimes the key to receiving physical healing from all stress and fear in the mind.

> *Beloved, I wish above all things that thou mayest prosper and be in health, even as thy soul prospereth.* (3 John 1:2)

The Lord begins our healing from the inside out. After our heart and soul are clean, then the body experiences healing. If fear is overwhelmed by hopelessness, then we are unable to pray, fast, and read the Word of God.

However, when we are weak and trying to overcome a weakness related to fear, the only safe place to be is in the will of God. Know that the Lord loves you and cares about your need. To overcome fear and weakness, ask God to remove it, quote the Word of God, obey His guidance, listen to the Holy Spirit, wait on God, praise Him before the answer comes, put the devil under your feet, and keep him there. For we know the devil came to kill, steal, and destroy, but Jesus came that we "might have life" and "have it more abundantly" (John 10:10). With God on our side and living inside of us, we can conquer and overcome all the fear that will attack us from day to day.

Another fear most people face is the fear of financial need, of life beneath their current standard. They fear living in bondage and never seeing themselves coming out, always going through one thing or another, wondering, *When will I come out?* The Bible declares that if you have faith as a grain of mustard seed, you can ask what you will, and you shall receive it. The key is believing it! Faith without works is dead; you can overcome this fear of financial need by believing the Word of God.

> *But my God shall supply all your need according to his riches in glory by Christ Jesus.*
> (Philippians 4:19)

Fear of not having adequate finances

He said in His Word that He will give us all His blessings if we will only observe and do His commandments.

And it shall come to pass, if thou shalt hearken diligently unto the voice of the LORD thy God, to observe and to do all his commandments which I command thee this day, that the LORD thy God will set thee on high above all nations of the earth: And all these blessings shall come on thee, and overtake thee, if thou shalt hearken unto the voice of the LORD thy God. Blessed shalt thou be in the city, and blessed shalt thou be in the field. Blessed shall be the fruit of thy body, and the fruit of thy ground, and the fruit of thy cattle, the increase of thy kine, and the flocks of thy sheep. Blessed shall be thy basket and thy store. Blessed shalt thou be when thou comest in, and blessed shalt thou be when thou goest out. The LORD shall cause thine enemies that rise up against thee to be smitten before thy face: they shall come out against thee one way, and flee before thee seven ways. The LORD shall command the blessing upon thee in thy store-houses, and in all that thou settest thine hand unto; and he shall bless thee in the land which the LORD thy God giveth thee. The LORD shall establish thee an holy people unto himself, as he hath sworn unto thee, if thou shalt keep the commandments of the LORD thy God and walk in his ways. And all people of the earth shall see that thou art called by the name of the LORD; and they shall be afraid of thee. And the LORD shall make thee plenteous in goods, in the fruit of thy body, and in the fruit of thy cattle, and in the fruit of thy ground, in the land which the LORD sware unto thy fathers to give thee. The LORD shall open unto thee his good treasure, the heaven to give the rain unto thy land in his season, and to bless all the work of thine hand: and thou shalt lend unto many nations, and thou shalt not borrow. And the LORD shall make thee the head and not the tail; and thou shalt be above only, and thou shalt not be beneath; if that thou hearken unto the commandments of the LORD thy God, which I command thee this day, to observe and to do them: And thou shalt not go aside from any of the words which I command thee this day, to the right hand, or to the left, to go after other gods to serve them. (Deuteronomy 28:1-14)

To sum it up, you have to overcome the fear of being afraid, and also the fear of not having and living below your standard and needs, because God's got your back!

CHAPTER THREE

BEHAVIOR ANXIETY:
THE FEAR OF UNCERTAINTY

F acing uncertainty and experiencing anxiety are part of life, as are moving, eating, and sleeping. As we are faced with unfamiliar challenges, we oftentimes prepare for the upcoming events, as is the case when we study for a test or speech. This is a result of behavior anxiety, which is the fear of uncertainty and anxiety, or fear, and the force to flee are a shield of protection from dangers. But these types of fears are not normal because when they become overwhelming and attack your daily living, they become an anxiety disorder. This could result in a mental illness disorder, as a result of being totally disabled and terrified of leaving home to go anywhere, which will keep you from becoming open to the world. God wants to help. As First Peter 5:7 says, "Casting all your care upon him; for he careth for you." Remember, beloved, you are not alone; God is on your side.

Many people face uncertain anxiety fear. These are some of the fears we face every day: 1) terror, dread, or fear of the unknown; 2) reverence or awe, or the fear of God; 3) a cause or grounds for fear, or a fear of things: cancer fear, heart attack fear, stroke fear, all kinds of sicknesses fear. These types of fears often have you worrying that something bad will happen to you and the ones you love, and this makes you feel impatient, irritable, and easily distracted. You will find yourself worried about life circumstances, all the time feeling terrified about what will happen. Remember, beloved, the thing Job feared most came upon him. But a lot of times, we bring things upon ourselves. This will leave you having fear of people watching you all the time, uncertain fear of losing control, or going crazy and losing your mind. Know this: God can give us peace of mind in whatever we are facing. He is all we need to make it.

Remember, you are not alone. We all face fear from time to time. Fear has existed since the beginning of time. Fear can be a good thing at times. For instance, when you fear getting a bad grade on a test, it can make you study more. But when fear holds us back, we need to conquer it with God's help

CHAPTER FOUR

WALKING OUT OF FEAR

Walking out of fear means you have overcome it, you have the victory over it. If you have won over fear, you can now say, "I have walked out of it." Regarding any kind of fear that had previously been attached to your mind, you can say, "I made it through. I have walked out of .... I am no longer going to accept the fear that comes to my mind. I have given it to my Lord and Savior, Jesus Christ, Who is the Author and Finisher of my faith. Who said, 'I will never leave you nor forsake you.' Who said, 'I will be with you even unto the end of the world.' Who said, 'Heaven and earth will pass away, but my word shall remain forever.' Who said, 'I am going away to prepare a place for you.' Who said, 'I am the Alpha and Omega, the beginning and the end.' Who said, 'I am that I am.' Who said, 'Hear me, for I am God.' Who said, 'You shall live and not die.' Who said, 'I am coming soon.' "

You see, you can walk out of fear and leave it in its place. Give it back to the devil because you've got power down inside of you. Remember, beloved, you are more than a conqueror. You have overcome. You have subdued. You have won by physical force to gain control over all, to gain favor over all and be victorious over all fear of doubt and unbelief. You can say, "I have won. I am a survivor. I have made it, and I am a conqueror," because the fight is already won by Jesus Christ. Jesus made it so that when He died on Calvary's cross—suffered, bled, and died for you and me—He gave you power over fear.

> *In God I will praise his word, in God I have put my trust; I will not fear what flesh can do unto me.* (Psalm 56:4)

All my fears for my God have girded me with strength over fear and strength to go to battle. I have the ability and strength to gain power over fear, given to me by the Holy Spirit. In Acts 1:8, the Bible declares, "Ye shall receive power, after that the Holy Ghost is come upon you." You've got power—power to say no and power to let it go! Power to do right! Power to do wrong!

Finally, my brethren, be strong in the Lord, and in the power of his might. (Ephesians 6:10)

For God hath not given us the spirit of fear; but of power, and of love, and of a sound mind.
(2 Timothy 1:7)

In God's hand is power and might, and in His hand is the power to make great, and to give strength and power to all.

Remember, beloved, you have power to overcome fear; it's all in your hand. You are a survivor of power, and you have walked out of fear.

God is my strength and power: and he maketh my way perfect. He maketh my feet like hinds' feet: and setteth me upon my high places. He teacheth my hands to war; so that a bow of steel is broken by mine arms. Thou hast also given me the shield of thy salvation: and thy gentleness hath made me great. Thou hast enlarged my steps under me; so that my feet did not slip.
(2 Samuel 22:33-37)

You see, beloved, you did not slip. You see, beloved, you are walking out of fear—and in God's Word. Fear not:

SURVIVING *your worst* FEAR

After these things the word of the LORD came unto Abram in a vision, saying, Fear not, Abram: I am thy shield, and thy exceeding great reward. (Genesis 15:1)

And the LORD appeared unto him the same night, and said, I am the God of Abraham thy father: fear not, for I am with thee, and will bless thee, and multiply thy seed for my servant Abraham's sake. (Genesis 26:24)

You see, you have no one to fear but God. Fear not, for the Lord is with you. Neither fear ye people. God wants you to fear Him and Him alone, and to keep all His commandments, that you shall not turn aside to the right hand or to the left. You shall walk in all the ways that the Lord your God hath commanded you, that you might fear the Lord your God to keep all His statutes and His commandments.

As long as God is with me, I can walk through the valley of the shadow of death:

I will fear no evil: for thou art with me; thy rod and thy staff they comfort me. Thou preparest a table before me in the presence of mine enemies: thou anointest my head with oil; my cup runneth over. Surely goodness and mercy shall fol-

*low me all the days of my life: and I will dwell
in the house of the LORD for ever.*
(Psalm 23:4-6)

You have nothing to fear! I am walking out of fear:

*In God I will praise his word, in God I have put
my trust; I will not fear what flesh can do unto
me.* (Psalm 56:4)

*Come and hear, all ye that fear God, and I will
declare what he hath done for my soul.*
(Psalm 66:16)

He has caused me to walk out of all my fear. He
has given me power to be more than a conqueror. He
has given me favor over fear. He has given me knowledge over fear. He has given me understanding over
fear. He has given me strength over fear. He has given
me joy over fear. He has given me increase over fear. He
has given me peace over fear. He has given me love over
fear. You see, God has given you all that you need over
fear to beat it when it attacks you in this day and time,
because He has overcome the world and has all power
in His hand—even power over life and death. You are a
winner! Psalm 34:9 says, "O fear the LORD, you His
saints; for to those who fear Him there is no *want.*"

CHAPTER FIVE

SURVIVING YOUR WORST FEAR

urviving your worst fear is overcoming fear within itself. Let's look at Job. Although he was an upright man, a perfect man, one who feared God, fear came upon him, but he continued to exist to outlast his fear. Job said, "All the days of my appointed time will I wait, till my change come" (Job 14:14). A man, having everything, went down to nothing. You can be up today and down tomorrow. Job, who had sores and boils all over his body, from the crown of his head to the soles of his feet, said, "What? shall we receive good at the hand of God, and shall we not receive evil?" (Job 2:10). Yet in all of this, Job did not sin with his lips.

For the thing which I greatly feared is come upon me, and that which I was afraid of is come

unto me. I was not in safety, neither had I rest,
neither was I quiet; yet trouble came.

(Job 3:25-26)

We as people of God have upheld the weak ones with His Word when they were falling, and we have strengthened them. But when the worst fear of your life is knocking at your door and is upon you, can you overcome it? If you are troubled, and fear is knocking at your door, and all your confidence and hope are gone, and you are left trying to survive the worst fear of your life, I tell you this: You need God! Nobody but God! Friends and family can't help. When everything is going wrong. Fear is overtaking you. Everywhere you turn is trouble, and you can't get ahold of your mind. It is gone every which way but loose. Can you survive this?

Let's look at Job. Job outlasted all his pain and suffering. He outlived it; he came through it all. And the Lord blessed Job; Job trusted in God! You can overcome your fear, just like Job. You can outlast your fears and outlive your fears. You can make it! And you will be a survivor!

If you really look at it, fear is all in our minds. You already have the victory over everything negative, including: always being on the defensive and putting up a stop sign, always thinking the wrong things, always thinking someone is out to get you or hurt you, not trusting yourself or anyone else, always looking for a way out, never wanting to face your problems or fears, always running, and so on. With these fears, you are only running from yourself. Psalm 48:6 says, "Fear took hold upon them there, and pain, as of a woman in travail." Psalm 56:4 states, "In God I will praise his word, in God I have put my trust; I will not fear what flesh can do unto me."

Remember, beloved:

The fear of the LORD is the beginning of wisdom: and the knowledge of the holy is understanding. (Proverbs 9:10)

The fear of the Lord is to hate evil, pride, and arrogance, and the evil way and the forward mouth do God hate. You see, you have to begin to hate fear and be not afraid of sudden fear, nor of the desolation of the wicked, when it comes, but be strong in the Lord and remember, God's got your back! So you don't have to fear your fear. If the Lord is on my side, I will not fear what people and things and circumstances can do to me because I know I can win with God. So I am getting rid of fear, and I am going to put on the whole armor of God, that I may be able to stand against the wiles of the devil.

When fear comes, beloved, remember what apostle Paul said:

For we wrestle not against flesh and blood, but against principalities, against powers, against the rulers of the darkness of this world, against spiritual wickedness in high places. Wherefore take unto you the whole amour of God that ye may be able to withstand in the evil day, and having done all, to stand. Stand therefore, having your loins girt about with truth, and having on the breastplate of righteousness; And your feet shod with the preparation of the gospel of peace; Above all, taking the shield of faith, wherewith ye shall be able to quench all the fiery darts of the wicked. And take the helmet of salvation, and the sword of the Spirit, which is the word of God: Praying always with all prayer and supplication in the Spirit, and watching thereunto with all perseverance and supplication for all saints ... (Ephesians 6:12-18)

Stand against fear because you can! You have the greatest One down inside you.

CHAPTER SIX

FACING MY
PERSONAL FEARS

When I was growing up, I developed one of my worst fears. I remember when I was about ten years old being on a school trip to the beach in Pensacola, Florida. At that time, I had a boyfriend (at least I thought I did). I sat with him on the bus, and he had me fooled. When we got to the beach, he acted as if he had it going on, at ten years old, as stated in my other book, *Then and Now: The Life Story of Bonnie Baker*. At that age, boys still had control over me, and I would do what they said. That day I faced my worst fear. We got to the beach, and he told me to go out into the water with him. Once I was in the water, he left me standing there and went back. All of a sudden, a big wave came, and under I went. He stood there and watched me go down and did nothing. As the lifeguard swam out to get me, I almost drowned. I had to be revived and get mouth-to-mouth resuscitation.

After I was revived, the fear of water became a very real fear for me—one that I never got over. Even now, I will not go underwater when I go swimming. I don't like to ride on boats or ships. We just got a cabin cruiser, and I've only been on it two times, and both times I had terrible seasickness. The second time, I was sick for two days and had to take medication (Dramamine) just to ride on the boat. That is one fear I still needed to conquer. I will tell you about that in Chapter 9.

Fear of drowning

Another one of my personal fears was dead people. I feared them all my life and did not want to be near them or see them. And I definitely did not want to touch them. Every time I went to see someone who had passed away, the devil would make me think the person was breathing, and I would think I could really see him or her breathing.

Another fear I had to conquer was going through an automatic carwash. The devil would make me think the water could come into the car and I would drown. I thought the brushes and rollers would come through the window and kill me as well. And I thought someone would be waiting to take me out when the car got to the end. While the car rolled through the automatic wash, I screamed and hollered as though someone had a gun and was trying to kill me. That was very frightening to me, but I conquered that fear!

And when I gave my life to the Lord Jesus Christ in 1982, He delivered me from that fear of dead people. After that, my grandmother passed away, as did my mother, my father, my father-in-law, and many friends and loved ones. I later was able to kiss and touch them all. I can be in the room with dead people by myself now. I don't know why I don't have the victory over my fear of water yet. I guess I need to really give it up to God and let Him deliver me totally, from my head to the soles of my feet, because this is one fear I really want to conquer. But like I said, I know it's only in my mind. And if I totally give it over to God, I know I can overcome it, just like all the other fears the Lord delivered me from.

But first I have to face my fear of going underwater head-on. I realize that I have never tried to swim underwater since I almost drowned. I am okay as long as my head is above the water. But I am going to have this testimony: I have overcome this as well! I am going to take swimming lessons to learn how to swim and go underwater, and then I will be able to swim like a fish. Glory to God! Hallelujah! Thank You, Jesus, because I am determined to win this one! I know it has been a long time, but I will conquer this one too! I am calling those things that aren't as though they were. I am shouting now for what is going to be. You will know because

Fear of swimming

I will be telling everyone, "Let's go swimming!" and then I will be able to say, "All of my personal fears are gone forever, never to return."

I talked to a few people, and here is what they said they feared, and, in many cases, conquered. My oldest sister, Barbara, had her four babies and got so sick she thought she was going to die. After giving birth to her baby girl, complications set in, and the fight was on for her life. But God brought her out. Another fear was when her husband was in the hospital and he had surgery; red-red blood was running out of him. The doctors had told her if they see red-red blood, then that is not good, and if they see dark blood, that is okay. The greatest fear of her life came upon her: that she would lose her husband and be alone. But God brought him out. However, about two years later, he died, and now the thing she feared the most has happened—she is alone.

I was talking to a mother who said every time her family is out shopping at the mall and her son needs to go to the bathroom, it's a problem because he has a fear of going into public bathrooms. This shows that age does not matter when fear attacks. One of my friends told me that after her mother passed away, she feared going to sleep at night, especially with her back turned to the door. This shows that fear can attack at any time. Another one of my friends was married for more than sixteen years and experienced a devastating divorce. While in the marriage, a spirit of fear attacked her, making her afraid of different sounds, closeness to some people, and certain places. She also experienced emotional fear, low self-esteem, oppression, and inner hurts and wounds, and it took several years of recovery to be delivered and set free. Deliverance came only through prayer and trust in the Lord and Holy Spirit through the Word.

Fear of being in dark surroundings

Surviving *your worst* Fear

Another friend said fear gripped her when she would come home from being out and go to open her door. Someone else feared taking showers when at home alone. Someone else said she feared the dark, and when she would get ready to go to work in the morning, it would

Fear of fire

be dark out. I have a friend whose worst fear was getting sick. Since age fourteen, she has feared sickness. She also overcame a fear of snakes, bugs, and mice. Someone else said one of her worst fears was being in a room by herself at night, and she had to pay her sisters to stay in the room with her. Someone else said she faced on a day-to-day basis a fear that she would suffocate, because she had been in a house fire, and she still has to have air constantly blowing in her house. Someone else is terribly afraid of fire. Another is afraid of her house burning down or of being burnt by fire.

Another one had a fear of driving again after having an accident. Someone else had a fear of crossing over bridges, any kind of bridge with water under it. This person would get on the floor of the car and panic and scream. Someone else had a fear of going to the movies or shows. Just being in a big, dark room was too much for that person. Another sister said she had a fear of having a close relationship with her mother or any other family member; she feared getting hurt. A child had a fear of going to school on the first day. Another child had a fear of taking pills because she thought they would get caught in her throat. Someone else feared being chased when she drove alone at night.

Many people have been hit by a moving train, trying to cross the road while walking or driving. Most people know that when the warning lights are flashing, you should stop and wait for the train to cross. However, many people take a chance—thinking they can outrun the train—and have lost their lives. Knowing that you can be killed by a moving train has caused many to have considerable fear at the train crossing.

Fear of being killed by a train

Someone else had a fear of going to the doctor. Another person had and overcame a fear of never getting married and dying at an old age, and now this person has been married for thirty-five years. Someone else

Surviving *your worst* Fear

Fear of loud noises, sounds, explosions

feared falling in love because this person got hurt when falling in love. Someone else fears failing tests that need to be taken for jobs. Another sister fears judgment day. This shows that fear can attack in any circumstance. Since 9/11, many people fear being in public places, afraid that a bomb will go off. This fear can manifest as a profound fear of loud noises.

But remember, beloved, God can deliver you from all your past and present fears. The thing that Job feared came upon him, but God brought him out and gave him back double for all he went through. You have nothing to fear but fear itself, and if you never face it, you can never get rid of it.

I was talking with someone who has a fear of never making it in life, or never amounting to anything. I know a sister in Christ who has God's hand on her life, and He wants to use her in ministry, but the fear of stepping out in God got a hold on her, and the fear won't let her accept the responsibility and obey God. Another sister in Christ told me she is so tired of being rejected all the time by people she loves. She said she is always trying to show love, but she always gets rejected, and the hurt and pain are so bad that when the love comes back to her, she doesn't believe that it's real, so she denies it.

Many people have been hit by a car, bus or truck. So, they have great fear when crossing the street.

Rejection is fear. And that is something we have to fight to win against, low self-esteem. Fear of worrying, fear of death, and fear of unbelief. Fear of pressure, fear of not fitting in, fear of wanting and having not, fear of talking, fear of being shut up in a box.

God gave me a vision concerning someone, and the vision He gave me centered on one big box. The box represented freedom. Up above it was a window, and on the side of it were three boxes—one small, one medium, and one large. Across from it was a big box that was a wall that had small circles inside it. Up above it was a tree, and the tree was dead. It had two branches on it that had stopped growing. It looked as though they had been cut off, like two small arms, and across from that were three boxes, all closed and dark.

Surviving *your worst* Fear

I began to write this down on paper as the Lord gave it to me. After I had written it down, I asked this person if she knew what the vision meant. She said no. This vision takes me back to "surviving your worst fear." Here you have a situation just like Job. The thing that this person feared came back upon her. God gave me the revelation to this vision.

> **She is free in this box**

Freedom

The first box represented her being free of everything before she got back inside the boxes.

The window

The window represented when she first began to look outside of what God had delivered her from, and these were all her fears.

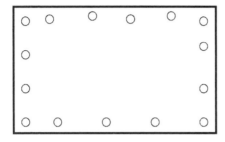

Wall of circles

The wall of circles represents when she began to put a wall up to protect herself from the fear she began to feel.

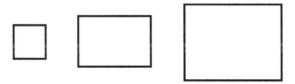

Back inside the boxes

These three boxes represent when she got back inside the boxes of fear but did not realize that the things she feared were about to overtake her again Remember, beloved, Job said, "The thing which I greatly feared is come upon me" (Job 3:25).

The tree

The tree represented when she stopped believing and trusting in God and her fruit began to die; doubt, fear, and unbelief then set in.

Three black boxes

The three black boxes represented when she got all the way back inside the boxes of fear and closed them up. The first small box began to grow, the next box got bigger, and then she was in the big box, and the fear was really growing. She closed the door to all the boxes, and now she is in the big box, where the fear has grown so big only God can bring her out of it.

Beloved, never doubt when God has brought you out because if the devil can get you back inside the box, closed off from everyone, he is not going to let you out again. God has given us power over fear; now let's use it! Greater is He that is in you than he that is in the world.

CHAPTER SEVEN

YOUR GREATEST FEAR

By Pastor Hattie White
Redeeming the Times Ministries
Greenville, North Carolina

I n the book of Job, we see that the thing Job feared the greatest was what came upon him and became a very real manifestation in his life that not only affected him, but his whole family. One of my greatest fears was losing my husband (his dying) and my job, which did happen, but the Lord brought me through it with a mighty hand. My husband had a massive heart attack on September 10, 1974, four days before our fourth wedding anniversary. I was devastated. He was in the hospital for about two and a half months, during which his chance of recovery was not good—a 40 percent chance of living a normal life. He was in ICU for most of that time. During this time, the Lord sent a pastor into his room to pray the prayer of salvation with him (this was when it was not looking so good for him), and although he was not yet convinced he wanted to serve the Lord (the timing of the Lord was not to come for him), he finally came out of the ICU and then home to have about five other heart attacks (up to the timing of his salvation). But God was preparing him to answer the call to salvation.

It was during those times that the enemy fought me concerning his ever having normal health, and whether he would die and leave me a young widow bringing up a small child. This was my greatest fear. The Lord saved him on June 24, 1977, on my one-year spiritual anniversary. He began to get better as he sold out to the will of the Lord, but in the back of my mind, the enemy kept fighting me about it every time my husband went to the doctor. According to all tests, his heart was only operating at 45 percent, and with only his main artery operating (the two smaller ones were completely blocked), the fear was real. For the most part, I put it aside as we grew in our walk with the Lord and began to trust Him. So for thirty-two years, it was great. My husband was my soul mate and the love of my life. We married right after I came out of high school.

Saturday, March 18, 2006, started out as another great day. We were awakened by our younger son, who needed to be on time for his first driving school lesson. So I got up to get ready to take him to meet the instructor, as my husband had broken his leg two weeks before. He was full of joy and laughter, teasing me about having my days mixed up because I had on green, and the day before was St. Patrick's Day. Then he asked me to cook him breakfast. Now, you must know I never did any cooking. All our married life, he did all the cooking, except at Thanksgiving and Christmas, when we would do it together, and I enjoyed it at those times. But I generally hated cooking; I would rather clean a house top to bottom. I didn't want to do breakfast, so I said, "Let me bring you some breakfast from 'Mickey D's.'" But he insisted I cook. He was laughing and just acting up. I said, "You need to stop acting up, or I won't cook it." He pretended to beg, so feeling bad, I went to cook a full breakfast for him, and he bragged and bragged about it, saying how good it was (not knowing it was going to be his last meal).

I said, "If you don't stop, it will be your last breakfast for a while from me." We hugged and kissed. I was leaving to take our son to his driving lesson. He asked me to go shopping because he wanted to study for the Sunday morning service message. When I was about fifteen minutes from the house, I received a call from our daughter, saying, "Mom, Dad said he doesn't feel good. He's going to go to the hospital to get checked out; he's short of breath and a little disoriented."

I called the house and asked him, "What's wrong? Do you want me to come back and spend more time with you? Did you change your mind about my going shopping?" He said no and told me to go on. He would be okay. I said, "No, I'll meet you at the hospital." Rescue got to the house in eight minutes (we checked the cell calls to and from the house), and when they got to the hospital with my husband, I went to him in the ambulance and asked if he was in pain. He replied no and said, "I'll see you inside."

Ten minutes later, the doctor came out to give me an update, and ten minutes after that, he came out to say they did all they could to save him, but they couldn't. Within five minutes of getting to the hospital, my husband went home to be with his Lord as a result of blood clots in both legs. This was my greatest fear. You see, we had been called to pastor six years prior to this happening. My world was over; my life was over. The only love of my life was gone. We did everything together; we went everywhere together; we were best friends. Surely this was not happening to me. *No, Lord, no! This has to be a dream; it has to be a dream!*

Thirty-six and a half years began to flash before me as I searched my spirit for answers. Why me? During the time of the funeral, I was not myself. I was just there. Thank God for my sister Bonnie, who came in from Michigan to help me out and made me eat when she got there. I began to feel better, but I was still lost.

I had just left him healthy and full of life and joy. Did I mention the fact that over the years, the Lord gave him a new heart, with X-rays to prove it? We had just built a new church after only three years of pastoring Redeeming the Times Ministries, and things were looking good. We were blessed, and the church was growing. "Why?" I asked the Lord, and His answer was, "I gave you thirty-two more years with him when I could have taken him with the first massive heart attack." All I could do was fall on my knees and worship and say, "True, Lord, thank You. And now help me walk through the pain."

Sometimes we get caught up in our fears, but all we need to do is just allow the Lord to help us get through those fears so we can say, "He has brought me through with a strong hand of victory."

About six months later, I lost my job after being there for twenty-nine years. But I knew why I lost my job: God was preparing me—little did I know—for full-time pastoring, and I am glad, although that's another one of my greatest fears. I am now happy to be done with that job because I am in the place where the Lord wanted me all along.

When we come to a pivotal point in the Lord or in our lives, our lives can change because of the fear of failing (in our marriage, that new job, the promotion at work, the new baby, the business we wanted for so long, etc.). Every paradigm shift in our lives brings a new challenge for us to deal with our fears. It's the fear from our subconscious mind that's trying to destroy us, or hinder us, and cause us not to trust in the revealed knowledge and will of God concerning His directing our steps.

As we take a look at fear, let us see how we can allow the Spirit of the Lord to bring our fear to the surface without it destroying us. For we walk by faith and not by sight. So we cast down imaginations and every high thing that exalts itself against the knowledge of God, and bring into captivity every thought to the obedience of Christ. We *must* practice the Word and do just as it directs us to do, and become doers of the Word of God and not just hearers with no change. The Holy Spirit will reveal to us what to release out of our heart so we can have fellowship with Him, undefiled. Negative meditations and imaginations only come to us by the enemy, to abort destiny, purpose, and the will of the Father in us as believers.

Fear is the opposite of faith, and it works in reverse in our negative consciousness because it's an area in which the Holy Spirit deals with us. Oftentimes we yield our members to the enemy to be used by him and not God.

> *Let the words of my mouth, and the meditation of my heart, be acceptable in thy sight, O LORD, my strength, and my redeemer.*
> (Psalm 19:14)

It is our subconscious that we must keep clean and pure and not contaminated by things that we entertain (things designed by the enemy to bring us into areas of contamination and condemnation oftentimes by way of the Internet, television, or any other avenue that can come into our mind, spirit, or subconscious that causes separation from the Lord, as far as His speaking to us in the Spirit)—which would be a great price to pay.

For the thing which I greatly feared is come upon me, and that which I was afraid of is come unto me. (Job 3:25)

Here we see that the things we entertain, meditate on, concentrate on, focus on, or fix our attention on can bring that fearful situation close to us, even to the manifestation thereof, because what we are doing in reality (practicing faith in the negative) in our spirit is bringing to pass negative things in our lives.

Hebrews 11:1 says, "Now faith is the substance of things hoped for, the evidence of things not seen." So we know that in the natural realm, things are not as they seem as we speak things or meditate on them. For as long as we have faith in God and believe on the thing that we speak, it shall come to pass.

Romans 4:17 states, "(As it is written, I have made thee a father of many nations,) before him whom he believed, even God, who quickeneth the dead, and calleth those things which be not as though they were."

Ephesians 3:20 declares, "Now unto him that is able to do exceeding abundantly above all that we ask or think, according to the power that worketh in us." So the things we think on—as well as the things we speak—do matter when we want to bring forth the right harvest. We were created in the image of our Father, and all things bring forth after their own kind. We need to be careful not to allow ourselves to abort His will by yielding to negative thoughts and things we *feel* in our spirit, things we dream, or idle or projected thoughts from the enemy.

We must stay free and not allow fear or the things we fear to control us, but instead yield to the Holy Spirit to guide us into the abundant life—by getting into a church with a pastor after the heart of God the Father, by developing a time of study (of the Word of God or some good books from the Christian bookstore that speak to your calling in the Lord), by investing in your relationship with the Lord. Be sure to get a very good study Bible. Stay around people who have a fasting and prayer life. Forsake not assembling with believers. You will need the strength of the body of Christ. The hearing of the Word will cause you to have faith and also cause you to transform your mind into the image of Christ.

Weapons of fear can come against you, but don't have to control you, so know that you can resist the enemy. If the fears in your subconscious have caused you some embarrassment or shame, or caused secret sins to manifest in your life, be honest about them, be transparent (in areas where you can be; it's not always viable), and deal with them so that they don't take over your or your family members' lives and cause generations of sin, shame, and strongholds.

The Lord will reveal areas in our lives where He will renew and transform us so we can have a peace of mind in our spirit to be able to worship Him and obey His voice.

So yes, fear is very real and must be dealt with. To be in denial is to let the enemy of our souls have the upper hand over us, and the cycle continues until a stronghold is built. It allows the enemy more access to our lives.

But the blood of Jesus applied to our lives can abort and stop the enemy from coming and going in our lives, where the Lord has set us free. So let us walk in the liberty of our Lord.

CHAPTER EIGHT

THE MANY FEARS
OF REJECTION

Rejection, which many people fear, means you are refused, denied, thought of as useless, or thought of as nothing. Fear of rejection gains control over your mind, body, and soul. Many people cannot handle rejection. Rejection can come from many avenues, such as your childhood, relationships, friendships, church family, family members, and many others. Many people fear that no one likes them, and they are alone and feel alone.

Others have a fear of people finding out a bad or crushing secret, having very low self-esteem, always not feeling good about yourself: *I don't look good. I am too fat. I am too small. I am too ugly. I eat too much. No one cares anyway. A spirit of fear has power over me. I fear I have lost the very one who loved me. I fear my loved one is*

*having an affair on me. I struggle with the pain of fear—
an unnamed fear that, if I talk about it, might happen to
me. I always feel very down about myself. I have a fear of
feeling I will never love like my friends do, a fear that I
will never have friends, a fear of not fitting in among my
peers, a fear of going outside, a fear of crowds, a fear of
being myself, a fear of never accomplishing my goals. I am
missing out because of my fear.*

Also, the fear of rejection prevents us from giving
and receiving truth. Fear makes it difficult to hear and
please God, and it keeps us from sharing the Word of
God. In Luke 17:25, we read, "But first must he suffer
many things, and be rejected of this generation." Jesus
also suffered from rejection and was denied.

These are some of the patterns of the fear of rejection: someone who does not believe anyone can love
him or her; someone who goes along with everything
and never says a word; someone who knows his or her
schedule is full but always says yes to make someone
else happy; someone who only says what other people
want to hear and puts on an act; someone who gives in
to peer pressure, like drugs, sex, or alcohol, just to fit in;
someone who takes comments too personally; and
someone who rejects God and His purpose in all that
He's done. What we should do instead of these negative
patterns is overcome rejection and show love in
response.

THE MANY FEARS OF REJECTION

Many times rejection can come from feeding on negative information about someone who doesn't like you, or thinking you will never be anyone important, or that your hair is too short, or that you don't wear the right clothes and they don't fit you, or that you talk too much, or that you don't know how to take care of business, or that you just can't do anything right and you always look so sad, or wondering why you always do something wrong, or why you always get your feelings hurt. Feeling rejected, feeling all alone, as if no one cares about you, is a bad place to be. You may be always thinking about hurting yourself to try and get back at the one who hurt you. Most of the time, this is a case for God because once you get that far gone, where you are feeling that everyone has let you down and no one is on your side, then you really need God.

Let your conversation be without covetousness; and be content with such things as ye have: for he hath said, I will never leave thee, nor forsake thee. (Hebrews 13:5)

Trust in the LORD with all thine heart; and lean not unto thine own understanding.
(Proverbs 3:5)

Casting all your care upon him; for he careth for you. (1 Peter 5:7)

SURVIVING *your worst* FEAR

Remember, beloved, when everyone else lets you down, you can always depend on and trust in God.

Psalm 115:11 says, "Ye that fear the LORD, trust in the LORD: He is their help and their shield." Psalm 115:13 states, "He will bless them that fear the LORD, both small and great."

All you have to fear is the Lord. Isaiah 12:2 declares, "Behold, God is my salvation; I will trust, and not be afraid: for the LORD JEHOVAH is my strength and my song; he also is become my salvation." All you need is God. Accept the fear of rejection that you are feeling and ask God to remove it. Quote the Word of God on it and receive it. It is easier than you think. Then, you will have freedom from your fears, and from negative feelings or thoughts. When you know they are different, and when the feelings or torments come to your mind, you can cast out all fear, doubt, and unbelief, and you can stand tall against the fear of rejection.

When you face the fear of failure, remember, this is another fear of rejection you have to push past. Take control of self-confidence, something that can make you feel good about yourself, happy, and free. First John 4:18 says, "There is no fear in love; but perfect love casteth out fear: because fear hath torment. He that feareth is not made perfect in love."

Because of personal rejection, when you feel afraid, your emotions take over and you say, "I don't even try to get people upset with me; it just happens all the time," "I just can't get anything right," "I face the fear of making decisions," "I fear changing my lifestyle," "I face the fear of making it successful." You see, what you need to do is break through all your negative thinking, raise up from low self-esteem, and push to a confidence level within yourself by creating momentum. To stay positive about yourself, defeat rejection by identifying the problem and overcoming it.

Overcoming fear can be tough during evangelism. When you are up speaking or teaching or preaching, you sometimes feel the rejection of the people. After you finish your talk, you can feel insecurity, shame, and personal rejection, not reception. It can make you feel very low inside. First Samuel 8:7 says, "And the LORD said unto Samuel, Hearken unto the voice of the people in all that they say unto thee: for they have not rejected thee, but they have rejected me, that I should not reign over them." Remember, you are not being rejected by God, so put your feeling under your feet and let God stand up in you.

Cry aloud, spare not, lift up thy voice like a trumpet, and shew my people their transgression, and the house of Jacob their sins. (Isaiah 58:1)

Here are some ways to overcome rejection:

- Know that you have a problem with rejection. Don't be afraid for what you know will happen. Tell yourself, "I can overcome the rejection or know when I hear it."

- Take control of your mind. The rejection starts in your mind, and it does something to you when you hear the words "You are a loser and will never win." You can be a winner! Tell yourself, "I will not be defeated!"

- If you are feeling driven by fear of a lack of appreciation, you have to learn to appreciate yourself first. Remember: It is a poor duck that does not praise his own pond. Learn to appreciate yourself. Even if no one will tell you, tell yourself, "I will make it." "I will have success." "I look good." "I will reject the pain that I feel." "I will accomplish my goal." "I will have." "I can love." "I can stand up and fight." "I can handle 'no' when I've been rejected." "I can handle the unexpected when it arrives." "I will handle the relationship when I have been let down." "I will handle the failure when it comes." "I will be able to handle the non-affection." "I will handle all the throwbacks when they come." "I will handle worries." "I will handle this loneliness." "I will handle low self-esteem." "I will walk in my positive change." "I do have the ability to overcome this fear of rejection."

CHAPTER NINE

CONQUERING MY FEAR

I n 2005, I went on a cruise. Never had I been on a boat that big before. It was very hard for me. My husband has always wanted to go on one. My two sisters and my brother-in-law were there the first night. I did not want to go out walking around or do much of anything. The next morning, we went for breakfast, and I found a table in the middle of the ship. After breakfast, my husband, my two sisters, and my brother-in-law went out on the balcony to sit and talk. I told them to go right ahead. I was okay, and one by one, they came back in to get me to go out on the balcony. When my brother-in-law came and said, "Come on, Bonnie, it's okay," I got up, trembling and about to get sick to my stomach.

I walked out and sat back against the window of the ship and talked with them. This took me all the way

Surviving *your worst* Fear

My victory cruise!

back to when I was a little girl in the fourth grade and almost drowned, and fear was still there, but glory be to God, on this cruise, I was determined to get past this fear. That fear had gripped me for more than forty-two years, and I thought to myself, *It's time to let this thing go.* After God saved me, I thought it was gone, but I found out it was still there. You see, you can carry things from your childhood into your adulthood and into your saved life and be bound by it—to the point that fear has a hold on you. So many times we pray about something and ask God to take it away, and we believe Him that it will be gone, but when it faces you, you realize you still have fear. Many people have different situations that they carry all their lives, and only God can deliver them. You see, you have nothing to fear but fear itself. I have found that out, and now I am more than a conqueror.

That night on the cruise, my husband had gone out of our cabin for a little while. Our cabin had an ocean view, and I looked out the window for a while. When I looked at the water, I began to get dizzy to the point that I thought I would fall, and as I looked way out into the water, I kept my eyes on the water, and then I began to look up. I was immediately reminded of Peter walking on water, and in the spirit, I could see it in Matthew:

And when the disciples saw [Jesus] walking on the sea, they were troubled, saying, It is a spirit; and they cried out for fear. But straightway Jesus spake unto them, saying, Be of good cheer; it is I; be not afraid. And Peter answered him and said, Lord, if it be thou, bid me come unto thee on the water. And he said, Come. And when Peter was come down out of the ship, he walked on the water, to go to Jesus. But when he saw the wind boisterous, he was afraid; and beginning to sink, he cried, saying, Lord, save me. And immediately Jesus stretched forth his hand, and caught him, and said unto him, O thou of little faith, wherefore didst thou doubt?
(Matthew 14:26-31)

You see, beloved, as long as you keep your eyes on Jesus and do not doubt, you can conquer your fear. That's why I was determined to conquer my worst fear. The first world was destroyed by water, and the devil knows it; he was in heaven when it was formed. And now he is on the earth, walking to and fro, seeking whom he may devour. But Jesus came that we might have life and have it more abundantly. Satan knows that if he can get fear down in you, then he's almost got you. But God says, "Keep your eyes on Me, and you can truly make it."

This was the beginning of a new experience for me, being delivered from my fear of water. Whatever your fears may be, keep your eyes on Jesus, and you can overcome them too.

I began to feel better and better, and the Lord spoke to me and said, "As long as you keep your eyes from looking at the water and look up, you can make it." Not only did I make it, but I conquered it all, and I did it that very moment. Realizing my fear of water had been conquered, I could hear in my spirit, It's all right now. I began to praise the Lord. I shouted in my cabin, thanking the Lord for delivering me.

The next day, we arrived at one of our stops, and we had to take a little boat across to an island. If I had not conquered my fear the night before, I would not have been able to get on that little boat, but it was all right then. I praised the Lord from that point on. I was outside on the balcony, close to the edge and looking over into the water. I tell you I thought I had it going on at that time. I said, "Look at me, look at me!" I began to act like a pro walking all around the ship, smiling and telling everyone I conquered this thing. Different people began to say, "We can see," and, "Thank You, Jesus."

Now every chance we get, I want to go on a cruise. We came home and got on our boat. We have a Bayline cabin cruiser that my husband and my girls try to get me to go on, and every time I would go before I conquered my fear, I would be sick for days and mess up the whole boat ride for my family. I complained so much about being sick that it got to be funny to them, and I could hear them on the top of the boat laughing and having a lot of fun. The girls would say, "Daddy, listen to Mama. She's about to throw up," and he would just say, "Oh, she'll be all right. Do you know if she took her pills before she got on the boat?" I was not able at the time to go and sit on the topside of the boat with the family. I had to go down in the deck, lie on the bed, and say, "Lord, help me, please. I am doing this for my husband and family because I know how much they love going for a ride on Sunday evenings after church."

I knew I would have to suffer the consequences of being sick and not feeling good for days, but I wanted to make my family happy. Now that I have conquered my fear, I can get on our boat and sit on the topside. PRAISE THE LORD! GLORY, HALLELU-JAH! THANK YOU, JESUS!

Surviving *your worst* Fear

Whether you have a fear of water, heights, rejection or something in between, you, too, can conquer all your fears. Whatever it is, trust God for it. He is here to deliver you if you want to be delivered. I had made up my mind that it was time to get past this, so we went on the cruise. I had to conquer this fear, and I did. And guess what, beloved? You can too!

ABOUT THE AUTHOR

Bonnie Baker, a little country girl from Vrenderburgh, Alabama, moved to Detroit in 1973. The Lord saved her in 1982 and called her into the ministry in 1985. Now she is totally sold out to the Lord. God has blessed her with the gifts of intercessory prayer, discernment of spirits, prophecy and interpretation, laying on of hands, preaching, and ministry of helps, among others. She married her husband, Dean, in 1983. They have four daughters—Tawana, Kenyatta, Chantel, and Lachisa—and nine children (three sons and six daughters) in heaven, as well as eighteen beautiful godchildren.

Bonnie has had much success since coming to Michigan. After writing the book *Then and Now: The*

SURVIVING *your worst* FEAR

Minister Dean Baker and Minster Bonnie Baker

Life Story of Bonnie Baker, she has opened three other businesses: her own mortgage company, Flash Mortgage Corporation; a health store; and a travel agency, Dean & Bonnie's Travel. In writing this book, God inspired her to tap into the spirit realm of "how we can be bound up by fear." Fear is a personal reaction, but it's still very real and something we create ourselves.

The only fear we as Christians should have is the fear of God. Fear can start in your childhood, and that is when we should try to get rid of it. This book will let you see that you don't have to struggle with fear anymore. In her last book, Bonnie told how God called her into the ministry, and now she's going all over the country preaching the Word of God to a dying generation, proclaiming that Jesus saves and will save you from all fear, doubt, and unbelief, and that God will deliver you out of any type of fear. She is indebted to do the will of God.

Be blessed in the name of the Lord. And remember, you have nothing to fear but fear itself.

Look for Bonnie's upcoming book,
Then and Now Part II.

AUTHOR CONTACT

Bonnie Baker
P. O. Box 74073
Romulus, MI 48174-0073